The Tao of Roark

Variations on a Theme from Ayn Rand

The Art of Living, Vol. 1

Peter Saint-Andre

I0087322

For other books by the author, visit
https://stpeter.im/

Published by the Monadnock Valley Press,
Parker, Colorado
http://www.monadnock.net/

Cover image by Tsvetomira Zaharieva

ISBN: 0615822959
ISBN-13: 978-0615822952

The Tao of
Roark

1. The Courage to Face a Lifetime

A young man rode his bicycle down a forgotten trail through the hills of Pennsylvania. The brilliant spring sun warmed him like a conscious caress. The leaves and trees and rocks called to him of the hope and promise of life on this earth. Alone in the wilderness, he felt the fresh wonder of an untouched world, where joy and reason and meaning were not only possible but a simple human birthright.

Some wondrous music of exaltation played in his head, the self-contained joy of endless variations spun out by an inexhaustible imagination. Yet in his life so far he had found precious few words or deeds or thoughts among the acts of men to match the meaning of that music. Not the work of man as a degradation of nature, but as an improvement upon given materials that could fulfill the promise of the earth. Not masters and slaves, but a free and independent life of mutual respect and voluntary interaction, without pain or fear or guilt. Not happiness and achievement served to him by others, but the straightforward sight of joy and reason and meaning made real, which would inspire in him the courage to create his own happiness and achievement.

He could give no name to the thing he sought.

He yearned for an exalted experience of life — but he was told that exaltation is reserved for things not of this earth.

He wanted human activity to be a higher step: something noble that he could respect, even something sacred that he could worship — but he was told that the only nobility and the only proper objects of worship exist above and beyond the merely human.

He longed to witness a spark of the divine in his fellow men, and to nurture that spark in himself — but he was told that aspiring to a share in the divine is the height of arrogance.

He hoped to find a way of life animated by a natural reverence for man and this earth — but he was told that the only path to spirituality lies in turning away from this life toward a supposed life after death.

He wished for some sign of what he sought, some guidepost on the road to joy and reason and meaning — but what he sought seemed perpetually just beyond his grasp.

The boy pedalled on through the quiet hills, revelling in the solitude and wondering about his future with the combination of agonized confusion, wistful longing, and passionate expectation that only youth can bring. On the trail ahead he saw a blue hole of open sky where the ridge ended and a valley began. He closed his eyes for a moment, suspending his sense of reality in the strange hope that at the top of the ridge he would find unobstructed sky above and below him.

When he reached the edge he opened his eyes to the most wondrous creation he had ever seen — a valley dotted with small homes that honored the earth and improved upon it by growing organically out of the ground, completing the unplanned beauty of the hills with an even greater beauty of human achievement and fulfillment.

Only after a long while did he notice a man sitting nearby — the man who had made this place real by designing the homes in the valley. Little did the man know that he had given the boy something beyond mere stone and glass: the courage to face a lifetime.

2. The Boy on the Bicycle

I was the boy on the bicycle.

Perhaps you were, too. Perhaps you, too, did something like ride your bicycle down a forgotten trail through the hills of Pennsylvania, wondering if you would find joy and reason and meaning in life. Perhaps you, too, embraced the solitude of your own companionship, treasuring each quiet hour of reflection in a noisy world, loving the very fact of being alone and alive, feeling an unbearable tenderness for the sight of this beautiful earth, breathing in the never-to-be-repeated singularity of your own personhood like great gulps of free fresh air, hungering for all the outstretched possibilities of what you might become — yet daunted by the enormity of the gap between your present and your future, and therefore seeking signposts on the road to a life you could in the end look back upon with the pride and honor of a job well done.

Perhaps in your seeking along that lonely path you came upon a novel entitled *The Fountainhead*. For a few days or weeks or months, it changed everything. Then you read the book again, perhaps a few times — challenged in your thinking, stirred in your emotions, deflected onto a new course, imbued with an incandescent fire, transported by a comprehensive vision of life as it might be and ought to be.

Perhaps, after the blinding flash of your first encounter with *The Fountainhead* had mellowed to the warm glow of enhanced awareness, new questions and challenges arose. Is this vision real? Can it be achieved in a world where joy and reason and meaning seem all too rare and elusive? Can I integrate these insights into my own life without submerging my individuality under a flood of ideas and abstractions that, however compelling, were created by someone else? Is Ayn Rand's philosophy not only an intellectual tradition of philosophical analysis and political advocacy, but also a wisdom tradition of spiritual maturity and personal enlightenment?

I, too, have asked these questions and faced these challenges. After more than thirty years of reflecting on *The Fountainhead*, I have gained some hard-won wisdom regarding the search for joy and reason and meaning in life.

I have tried my best to distill and condense that wisdom into this short book.

That I have done so through a set of variations on a theme from *The Fountainhead* no more makes me a spokesman for Ayn Rand than the *Rhapsody on a Theme of Paganini* made Rachmaninoff a spokesman for his Italian predecessor. The theme here is Rand's, but the voice in the variations is my own — a salute to Rand across the chasm of time.

Yet the model for this work is not the orchestral extravagance and lush harmonies of Rachmaninoff's *Rhapsody* but the single instrument and contrapuntal austerity of Bach's *Goldberg Variations*. This two-part introduction, a paean to joy and reason and meaning, is the songful aria that establishes the theme. In what follows, I explore many variations on that theme; yet, as with Bach, the variations are built not on the melody of the sarabande but on the prosaic, unnoticed, but foundational bass line — with canons and fugues and arabesques sometimes taking the music far from the original notes. After these harmonic excursions, the aria reappears in several restatements of the theme: a hymn to love for existence, the light within, and the meaning of life in what I call the Tao of Roark.

I have worked to maintain a light touch at the keyboard, serious but not preachy, because it is not my place to tell you what you "should" or "ought" to think or choose or do or feel. I have presented the Tao of Roark in the first person to make it clear that these are my thoughts, and that I would not dare to replace your own processes of observing, experiencing, thinking, and reflecting. Indeed, at root, I have written this book almost entirely for myself: to determine how I want to live my life, to clarify for myself what I mean by a philosophy for living on earth, to select the values that I deem most important, to enlighten myself about what really matters in life, to inspire myself to reach the highest form of excellence, to create and enjoy something beautiful and uplifting in a world that is too often ugly and small.

Despite the fact that this book is something private and precious and intimately personal, I have chosen to make it public in the hope that you, too, will find some wisdom here for yourself.

3. Joy

Howard Roark laughed.

When faced with expulsion from engineering school and the end of his dream of becoming an architect, he didn't whine or complain. He didn't get angry. He didn't blame his misfortune on the government or the schools or the culture at large. He didn't plead with the dean for reinstatement. He didn't worry or fret. He didn't collapse in fear and despair over his career prospects. He didn't even start thinking and planning about what to do next.

No.

Instead, he went for a long walk to his favorite swimming hole, took off his clothes, and dove down into the cool deep waters to enjoy himself and relax.

And, because he wanted to, he laughed.

4. Reason

Working like a convict in the unbearable heat and dust and noise of a granite quarry in midsummer, Howard Roark glanced up to see the incongruous sight of an elegantly dressed woman on the cliff's edge above him. Their eyes met and immediately he knew with intimate, wordless, flagrant understanding that he meant more to her than any man she had ever met, that he caused in her an overwhelming feeling of both shame and pleasure, that she wanted him to take ownership of her in the most masterful, degrading, scornful way possible. From that first glance, they shared a secret, unspoken understanding that she was openly inviting him to rape her.

This may be many things — passion, fire, drama, force, power, will, intuition, insight, projection, mania, lust, intoxication, infatuation, madness — but it is not reason.

Reason is what Roark displayed in his buildings: their logical economy of plan, their organic integration with the site, their crystalline efficiency, their supreme respect for the inhabitants, their comprehensive integrity of design.

Unfortunately, it is much more difficult to build those qualities into my relationships and my own character than into stone and glass.

5. Meaning

Howard Roark and Gail Wynand walked together at the crest of a hill on Wynand's estate in Connecticut. Roark tore a thick branch from one of the trees, grabbed both ends, and bent it slowly into an arc. And he said: "Now I can make what I want of it: a bow, a spear, a cane, a railing. That is the meaning of life."

Wynand, seeing Roark's wrists and knuckles tensed tightly against the resistance of the living green wood, recognized immediately the meaning of his own life. So he asked: "Your strength?"

But strength and power were not the meaning of life for Roark, whose singular focus was to create uniquely original and integrated buildings that would change the shape of things on this earth, for himself and for no one else. Thus he answered: "Your work."

6. The Soul

In her marriage to Peter Keating, Dominique Francon was perfectly selfless: she displayed no initiative, no desire, no independence, no will, no self, no soul. But what is the self or the soul? It is the thing inside me that thinks, values, makes decisions, and feels.

Roark knew this, too. As he said in his courtroom defense, the functions of the self are to think, to judge, to act, and to feel.

Thought, choice, action, and feeling. In these four human powers, properly understood, can be found a complete philosophy of living.

This insight provides the basis of the Tao of Roark — the foundation for my harmonic explorations — the bass line upon which I build my variations.

7. Thought

The power of thought is my ability to use my mind to understand reality.

Thought involves awareness, perception, focus, clarity, objectivity, independence, honesty, integrity, a firm foundation in the facts of reality, a fine-tuned receptivity to the way things are, the passionate pursuit of passionless truth — yet also empathy, understanding, patience, and the ability to grasp the personal context of those I interact with.

Thought is not only logical, intellectual, or mathematical — it can be musical, literary, visual, spatial, mechanical, organizational, social, interpersonal. Its raw materials are curiosity, imagination, creativity, looking ahead as well as looking back, and faithfully attending to what is present before me. It results not just in knowledge but in wisdom, perspective, insight, and enlightenment.

8. Choice

The power of choice is my ability to direct my energy and attention toward what I find interesting and important in life.

Choice means taking responsibility for my thoughts and actions and feelings, directing the course of my life, having and pursuing my own purposes, relying on my own perception of the truth, bowing to no one's will but mine except through my own free assent, honoring the absolute sovereignty of those around me, and pursuing only voluntary interactions in my life and in society.

Choice implies self-respect in the deepest sense: honoring what I hold to be important, having strength of will and the courage of my convictions, giving my attention to what interests me, devoting my life energy to that which matters most, trusting in my evaluations, spending my precious time on tasks that are consistent with my values, doing what brings me happiness, concentrating on ways to create significant value in the world, focusing on what is under my control and ignoring what is not under my control, seeking to master myself but not anyone else, and never letting go of my vision of what is possible to me.

9. Action

The power of action is my ability to create value in the world.

The domains in which I can create value and achieve something good are many and diverse: my work, my family, my health, my character, my friendships, my community, and my avocations are primary among them.

Achievement, too, takes many forms: I create value not only if I am a great innovator but also if I incrementally improve an existing technique, if I add to the stock of human knowledge and culture, if I provide a valuable service, if I raise good children, if I strengthen the bonds of mutual respect in my friendships or community or society, even if I only preserve and maintain the good things that were created by those who came before me; indeed, I can gain or keep value in relation to any object, creation, service, process, relationship, art, science, technique, activity, or field of human endeavor.

Further, the good is almost infinitely variable, because any positive value is good: whatever is useful, pleasant, efficient, competent, skilled, masterful, beautiful, elegant, logical, clear, healthy, clean, helpful, humane, wise, loving, kind, courageous, independent, rational, honorable, respectful, dignified, tasteful, joyous, exuberant, passionate, spontaneous, creative, inventive, intelligent, honest, direct, strong, fearless, free, voluntary, serene, innocent, blameless, or integrated is, all other things being equal, good and valuable.

To love the creation of value is to have a boundless energy, a joyous restlessness, a deep intrinsic motivation — it is to achieve an effortless flow of action, a seamless harmony of work and play, a state in which my own person vanishes into the background because I am supremely immersed in the doing.

10. Feeling

The power of feeling is my ability to experience the emotional meaning of my thoughts, choices, and actions.

Yes or no, for me or against me, positive or negative, life-enhancing or life-threatening, pleasant or painful, a benefit or a cost, a source of joy or of suffering — at root my capacity to feel is a unique source of feedback about the way I live my life. And, because my life is irreducibly individual, I can find that awareness only through my own emotions. The knowledge I gain comes from how I use my power to think, the direction I take comes from how I use my power to choose, and the value I create comes from how I use my power to act. Those achievements have a direct effect on how well I succeed at the task of human living, which I measure fundamentally by my enjoyment of life. Thus joy is not a mere surface phenomenon, but something deep and serious: it is the benefit that all my efforts go to pay for, the cash value of honoring my true interests in thought and choice and action.

Yet holding joy as an ideal does not mean that I refuse to acknowledge painful facts or experiences. Life can hurt, and the reality of loss is all too often with me. The capacity for joy is but the most positive realization of my capacity for feeling and emotion, and I must nurture that more fundamental capacity if I am to find the greatest joy in life. The actions and creations that I love most exhibit an openness to emotional experience. At its best, that experience is positive; but being open to experience means not shrinking from the negative, either.

Further, my emotions are not only positive or negative, on or off, white or black; they can be tremendously subtle. Consider the differences of intensity, depth, and energy between being calm or serene, cheerful or exuberant, satisfied or fulfilled, involved or engaged, interested or passionate, happy or ecstatic. Because emotions are a form of awareness, attending to these subtle differences can create a profusion of color in my life.

Finally, not all of those colors need to be fiery and intense. Although Rand's novels celebrate the highest passions, they also underline the importance of less ardent emotions: the sense of family that Roark and Henry Cameron feel in performing a daily routine together; the tenderness of Roark silently placing his hand on the shoulder of the night watchman at Cortlandt Homes; the firm sympathy and complete understanding that Roark extends to Steven Mallory when he needs it most; the bonds of trust, good will, and brotherhood that Roark and Mike Donnigan feel for each other; the fact that the employees in Roark's architecture office experience him as warm, approachable, and deeply human; the young, kind, friendly laughter that comes from Roark when he is talking with Peter Keating about their chosen profession; the natural joy and mutual confidence that Mallory, Donnigan, and Roark experience when they are together; the quiet satisfaction that Roark feels about having designed a building (even if, like his Stoddard Temple, it is disfigured beyond recognition).

11. Harmony

Roark's rule of building is this: "Nothing can be reasonable or beautiful unless it's made by one central idea, and that idea sets every detail. A building is alive, like a man. Its integrity is to follow its own truth, its one single theme, and to serve its own single purpose."

Yet the integration Roark describes is more literary and aesthetic (making my life a work of art) than human and practical (being successful at the great task of living).

What level of integration is possible to me as an individual?

At root, it is the harmony of thought, choice, action, and feeling.

Integrating thought into choice, action, and feeling means that my knowledge is not an idle curiosity or an end in itself. Instead, I use what I learn about the world and myself as a firm basis for the choices I make, the direction I take, the people and things I attend to, the activities on which I spend my time and energy, the areas in which I focus, the things I judge to be within my span of control or influence, even the feelings and emotions I consider to be healthy and justified. When I integrate the power of thought into all aspects of my life, I achieve a great clarity, like the parting of the clouds revealing a radiant blue sky.

Integrating choice into thought, action, and feeling means concentrating my efforts at learning in areas that are congruent with my nature and my interests, taking seriously the responsibility to use my mind and weigh the evidence of my senses and draw my own conclusions, focusing my time and energy where I can have a significant impact on the world around me and within me, taking a systematic approach to realizing my values and decisions in action, evaluating what I know and do and feel in the light of what is important to me — and adjusting my direction in life accordingly. When I integrate the power of choice into all aspects of my life, I achieve a great simplicity, like the pure spirit and breath of every natural living thing.

Integrating action into thought, choice, and feeling means connecting what I learn and know back to the practical concerns of living, always preparing myself physically and emotionally for the realization of my ideas and choices in action, studying methods for becoming more productive and creative, increasing my competence and mastery in my chosen profession and the other pursuits that matter to me, actively investing in friendships and relationships that might bring me joy, choosing values that I can realistically achieve, cultivating thoughts and feelings that lead to successful action (and pruning those that don't), focusing my energy and attention on the value that I want to create in life. When I integrate the power of action into all aspects of my life, I achieve a great abundance, like a fertile valley overflowing with life.

Integrating feeling into thought, choice, and action means attending carefully to my emotional reactions, honoring my emotions as a form of awareness that yields evidence about myself and my values, using the possibility of joy as a great motivator for action, valuing the honesty of my feelings as a true indicator of how successful I have been in my thoughts and choices and activities, learning to enjoy what is good and valuable so that my ideas and values and feelings are a seamless whole. When I integrate the power of feeling into all aspects of my life, I achieve a great tranquility, like the serenity and peace of the earth at dawn.

This depth of inner harmony is hard to achieve. I do not need to also introduce the notion of integrity as a single theme or purpose that sets every detail of my life. Thus I pursue that which is humanly achievable, not that which is impossible to me.

12. Objectivity

Objectivity is hard.

To be objective is to focus on the way things are, not the way I wish things would be. It is to recognize the facts of reality, no matter how difficult and unpleasant they are. It is, as Thoreau said in *Walden*, to work my way through the mud and slush of opinion, prejudice, tradition, delusion, and appearance, until I come to the hard bottom of rocks in place, which is reality. It is to admit as true only that which corresponds to the facts as I have worked to perceive them, clearly and without illusion. I call this clear perception "the track of truth".

To be objective is to be aware of the many ways I can stray from the track of truth: that I am drawn to evidence confirming what I already believe, that I seek out those who agree with me, that events can prime me to accept ideas that might be in error, that I am overconfident about the extent of my knowledge, that I presume to know when I don't, that I jump to conclusions, that I succumb to the power of symbols, that I am tempted to hew to party lines and cave in to peer pressure, that I follow fads and fashions all too easily, that I overvalue the insights of those within my group, that I want to believe things that are beautiful or exciting or consistent with the rest of my beliefs, that the seductions of ideology can blind me to the facts of reality, that I desire knowledge without process and insight without effort, that few things are more difficult than honoring the considered judgment of my own mind.

To be objective is to know that these snares and traps and idols apply to everyone, but that I especially am not immune from them, so that I must expend great energy to resist them. It is to have the childlike simplicity of accepting events as if they cannot be changed, to recognize what is within my span of control and what is outside it, to know that I can control and possess only myself, not anyone or anything else. It is to immerse myself in facts: in science, in history, in statistics and numbers, in the evidence of my senses, in art as a created object. It is to pay close attention to these things, to really see and hear and know them, to think clearly about them without preconceptions.

When I am objective, I stay on the track of truth: I recognize its faintest signs in the undergrowth of physical reality and human culture, I quietly attune myself to its voices and musics and rhythms through all the noise and chatter of society, I feel its finest textures in my fingertips, I even sense when the lack of it smells wrong or leaves a bad taste in my mouth. Many are the manifestations of truth, and by turns I must be subtle, direct, serene, and bold to grasp them.

13. Honesty

Honesty is the essence of objectivity in a social context.

Honesty is my recognition that you too are a thinking being, that you too have the same cognitive relationship to the world that I do, that you too have the same desire to know that I do, that both of us are focused on the same reality and thus will likely come to similar conclusions if you and I both use our powers of thought.

My honesty enables you to be more objective. Your honesty enables me to be more objective. Indeed, my honesty also enables me to be more objective, because it instills in me a habit of truthfulness. By being honest with each other, you and I build a shared commitment to recognizing reality and sustain a shared culture of achieving objectivity.

14. Self-Knowledge

Objectivity about myself is hardest of all. Its many meanings are captured in the phrase "Know Yourself", inscribed at the ancient temple of Delphi and part of the core wisdom of classical civilization.

To know myself means to know my measure, my limits, my powers, my abilities, my special talents; to know my strengths and weaknesses; to know my place, my role, my context, my calling; to know what I can and cannot do; to know what I can and cannot be; to know the limits of my knowledge and wisdom, what I know and do not know; to know what I truly want in life; to know the name of my soul, my real identity, my true self; to know how easy it is to sell my soul and how hard it is to keep it; to know human nature; to know divinity.

And to know myself means to know, finally, that it is hard to know all this because self-deception is the easiest thing in the world.

How to attain self-knowledge? There are many paths: knowledge of anthropology, sociology, psychology, biology, and evolution; reading of history and biography; experience of novels, drama, music, poetry, painting, sculpture, and the other arts — even creation of such works where I am able; immersion in physical disciplines such as the martial arts; exploration of philosophies, religions, and spirituality; observation, experimentation, action, cooperation, and the exercise of all my faculties; mentorship and teaching; love and friendship; meditation, reflection, and solitude.

I walk as many of these paths as I can. They are tools that can help me gain objectivity about myself. Yet even with these tools in hand, I know that it is harder to be honest about myself than about anything else in the world.

15. Responsibility

Responsibility is hard.

To be responsible is to be held answerable and accountable for my actions, because a full, objective account of what has happened needs to include what I did or didn't do.

To be responsible is to understand and accept myself as a cause of what happens in my life. Not necessarily as the only cause, but certainly as the primary cause. It can be difficult to remain objective about the degree to which I am a cause for any given event or its consequences, for I tend to attribute my successes to myself, and my failures to others and to external circumstances.

To be responsible is to govern my thoughts, my choices, my actions, and my feelings. Thus responsibility is a form of self-governance, and a precondition of freedom; for great freedom imposes great responsibility.

Responsibility looks back at what I have done, but it also looks ahead — for if I am responsible then I shall choose and act with the expectation that I might need to answer for what I do. Thus a sense of personal responsibility induces deliberation, caution, prudence, consideration, careful planning, even good manners.

When I am responsible, I walk a consistent path and I have a consistent aim in life. I have integrity, constancy, solidity, coherence, harmony, wholeness. By being true to myself and my principles, I become someone who is worthy of honor, trust, and respect.

There is much work involved in taking full responsibility for my life: I must learn and apply how to succeed in my chosen profession, how to maintain my health, how to save and invest for the future, how to defend myself and my family, how to be a good friend to those I care about, how to build a strong relationship with my partner in life, how to think clearly, how to make good decisions, how to be productive and creative, how to communicate effectively, how to cultivate my inner life, how to exercise self-control and achieve self-mastery, how to continually improve myself as a human being. Although it is tempting to think that I can depend on someone else to do these things for me — my family, my friends, a service I hire, a company I work for, a government agency, a charity that will help me in my time of need — the harsh truth is these tasks are primarily my responsibility and mine alone.

16. Respect

Respect is the essence of responsibility in a social context.

Respect is my recognition that you too are a choosing being, that you too must make your own decisions and select your own values and achieve your own happiness, that you too have the same desire that I do to succeed in living a fully human life.

If I am a good and worthy person, the prospect of earning my respect challenges you to become more responsible and to live up to your highest standards. If you are a good and worthy person, you inspire greater responsibility and moral ambition in me. Earning respect is not living second-hand, as long as I choose to interact with those I can honestly respect and admire. Calling each other to responsibility is one of the great values of friendship; yet here too my actions can also influence the broader culture of interactions I have with all people, not only those who are dear to me.

There is a beautiful Sanskrit word that captures the essence of such respect: *namaste*. It means: "the divine in me honors the divine in you".

17. Self-Trust

Just as I am the easiest person to deceive, so I am the hardest person to trust.

To be trustworthy inside and out, I must have great command of myself, great mastery of my emotions, great loyalty to my principles, great constancy of purpose, great internal discipline. I must keep straight, guide myself, monitor myself, point myself in a consistent direction, set my own path in life, live up to my ideals, and aspire to the highest excellence I can achieve.

To be trustworthy inside and out, I must have a strong moral compass within me, and not merely respond to pressures and sanctions that come from outside of me. I must choose my own principles and command my own laws, for myself alone and for no one else. I must be sovereign, autonomous, and a more strict governor of my own actions than any external force could ever be.

To be trustworthy inside and out, I must do what I want. As Peter Keating observed, this is not the easiest thing in the world but the hardest: to know what I truly want, what is best for me, what is consistent with my highest potential — and then to have the courage of my convictions by working tirelessly to achieve that in my life.

To mine own self be true — this requires deep self-knowledge and great self-discipline. Self-respect, self-esteem, self-consideration, and self-love are secondary effects — feelings that can only be based on the hard-won reality of self-worth. I must not confuse the cause and the effect.

18. Productivity

Productivity is hard.

To be productive is to create or preserve what is valuable and important, to achieve something significant in my life.

If I am to be productive, I must focus on my priorities, concentrate on high-value activities, channel my values and choices into achievable tasks and concrete actions, and be disciplined about my time and my life — for there is no self-direction without self-discipline.

When I create something of value, I close the gap between wish and fact, between the ideal and the real. By no means does this happen all at once; depending on what I want to achieve, it can take months, years, even decades to realize my goals, to make my values real in the world — with many setbacks and obstacles and challenges along the way. Patience and persistence are essential to my success.

Productivity is not a duty, but a desire for something higher and greater in my life: a matter of aspiration, passion, and energy applied to the great task of making my values real on this earth. At root, productivity is an expression of love, for to be a person who gets things done I must above all love the doing.

19. Collaboration

Collaboration is the essence of productivity in a social context.

Collaboration is my recognition that you too are an active being, that often you and I can achieve more together than apart, that often the creation of value is not a solitary pursuit but a matter of mutual achievement, focus, discipline, energy, and aspiration — a matter of being drawn together toward a shared goal in a shared pursuit based on shared values.

There are many challenges here. If there is no self-direction without self-discipline, is there also no shared direction without shared discipline? How can I respect your individuality within a group effort? It helps that you have your own domains of expertise and I have mine, that you and I can divide up the work so that you have your tasks and I have mine — but you and I always face the dangers of groupthink, of hierarchy, of power, of holding the organization above the individual. I must continually be mindful of these dangers if you and I are to work together with mutual respect and complete voluntarism.

20. Self-Improvement

My most challenging project is myself.

No area of possible achievement involves greater obstacles, difficulties, and resistances than my own soul. Yet no area offers greater potential rewards.

Self-improvement is soul-improvement: being productive of my character. I can improve my mind, my body, my decisions, my emotions; I can pursue excellence that is intellectual, physical, financial, ethical, professional, cultural, spiritual; I can be morally ambitious, I can define and refine my moral compass; when I make mistakes I can realize them, admit them, and correct them; I can seek discipline and control and mastery over myself, I can focus my self-knowledge and personal responsibility into internal action through superior habits of thought and choice and feeling.

Self-improvement is a matter of improving, not remaking. If I seek to improve, I accept myself as the foundation; I see myself as material for action; I build upon what I already am. I do not raze the site upon which I shall build my life; instead I integrate my building with the site, just as Roark did with the homes he designed.

Roark is a law of nature, perfect and complete from his earliest youth. Yet I was not born perfect: every day I must grow and improve in my character. Only slowly and with hard work will I reach the highest point of my completed being. As Baltasar Gracian says in *The Art of Worldly Wisdom*, I will know that I have achieved the full round of my excellences by the clearness of my thought, the maturity of my judgment, the firmness of my will, and the purity of my taste.

The true result of self-improvement is not self-esteem, because a mere feeling about myself is never primary. No, it is something much harder to achieve: self-value and self-worth.

21. Passion

Passion is hard.

To be passionate is to love this earth and everything in it, to love my life, to be devoted to my values and ideals, to be fully engaged with the world, to take my life and my soul seriously, to never give in to despair, to always hold on to a great sense of hope and if necessary to make my own hope, to provide the motive power in my life, to be thankful for all that I experience, to care deeply about making the world a better place through my thoughts and choices and actions.

If I am passionate about my life, I don't float through it — I live with attention, engagement, awareness, curiosity, interest, devotion, energy, immersion, enthusiasm, motivation, commitment, depth of feeling, moral ambition, love for my values, love for existence, and reverence for life in all its forms.

22. Compassion

Compassion is the essence of passion in a social context.

Compassion is my recognition that you too are a feeling being, that you too experience the emotional meaning of life in irreducibly individual ways, that you too are capable of pleasure and pain, joy and suffering, triumph and tragedy — that you too have opened yourself to great feeling and to the vulnerability such openness brings.

Can I give you empathy without pity, understanding without condescension, attentiveness without influence, commitment without exclusion? Can I help to bring out the best in you without seeking to direct your life? Can I see what is best for your life without seeking to impose it upon you? Can I treat all people with humanity, some with fellowship, fewer with friendship, fewer still with great love — without falling prey to the traps of in-groups and out-groups, judging without individual understanding, and the false alternative of deification versus demonization? Can I use my broad understanding of life not as a means to ignore your context but as the basis for treating you with presence and perspective? Can I feel great joy in your success while remaining independent in my own happiness? Can I see my relationships as a source of great value without basing my self-worth on the approval of others? Can I give my love precisely because those I love are not my chief reason for living?

These are the challenges of compassion.

23. The Inner Life

The hardest passion to accept is my passion for myself; the most difficult person to love is myself; the attention I most resist is directed within.

To experience life inside myself, I must accept my feelings as signs and signals of what I truly value, I must take clear perception as a precondition of strong feeling, I must listen to myself and train myself to hear, I must attend to the fine gradations of my emotional experience.

The inner life involves true joy in the senses, for seeing and hearing and touching and tasting are deeply human ways to know and love what is.

When I cultivate my inner life, I attend to myself; I am not afraid to be alone, indeed I revel in solitude and I enjoy my own companionship.

Can I be a friend to myself? Can I honor myself? Can I be self-contained yet still reach out to others and to the world at large? Can I grant myself compassion and empathy and understanding while never giving up my drive for self-improvement? Can I love myself in the toughest and tenderest ways possible, and strive above all to be worthy of such reverence? Can I hold onto my dreams, hopes, ideals, aspirations, deepest interests, and inner passions? Can I refuse to float on the surface of life but instead dive deep within myself in a search for individual freedom, personal dignity, spiritual depth, and moral beauty? Can I do all this without pretension, with simplicity and seriousness and humility and a realization of how far I have yet to go in my search for joy and reason and meaning?

24. Inner and Outer

The first great integration I can achieve is an inner harmony of thought, choice, action, and feeling. The second great integration I can achieve is a harmony between my inner life and my outer life.

My inner life and my outer life are two aspects of the same achievement. To consistently track the truth implies that I am equally honest with myself and with you, that I equally seek knowledge of reality, of other people, and of myself. To consistently honor self-direction means that I choose my own direction in life and also that I respect the direction you have chosen for yourself. To consistently create value implies that I create value in the world through my work, that I create value in my relationships with other people, and that I create value within myself by improving my habits and my character. To consistently experience meaning implies that I am passionate about my own life and compassionate about the lives of others.

If I am to recognize and respect the powers of thought, choice, action, and feeling in myself, I must recognize and respect them in you. Those I interact with, those I work with, those I befriend, those I love, all are thinking, choosing, acting, feeling beings. I must respect their intelligence, autonomy, experiences, activities, emotions, perceptions, insights, choices, and freedom. And further: I have a great opportunity to learn from the people in my life through mutual work, trade, inquiry, friendship, and love.

The same principles apply whether I am facing inward or facing outward or walking side by side with you. To live with integrity is to be of one piece, to be faithful in all I do to my best self and to the name of my soul.

This great integration is the harmony of the inner and the outer.

25. Self and Other

Understanding others is knowledge, but understanding myself is enlightenment; mastering others is power, but mastering myself is strength. Therefore in knowledge there is power, but in enlightenment there is strength.

Being selective about others is preference, but being selective about myself is simplicity; experiencing others is pleasure, but experiencing myself is depth. Therefore in preference there is pleasure, but in simplicity there is depth.

Knowledge, power, preference, and pleasure are signs of desire; enlightenment, strength, simplicity, and depth are signs of purpose.

When I focus primarily on controlling others or seeking their approval, I live second-hand and thus I am on the path to desire, dissolution, and dependence. When I focus primarily on improving myself, I live first-hand and thus I am on the path to purpose, integrity, and autonomy.

26. To Think and Not to Think

Honoring the power of thought brings me great enlightenment, but sometimes greater enlightenment comes from not thinking.

Sometimes I have thought everything I can think for now, as Howard Roark did when went for a swim at the quarry instead of planning the next phase of his life.

It is pointless to think and plan far beyond the horizon of my lifespan. History provides valuable perspective, but I cannot change the past. Envisioning the future helps me navigate my direction in life, but the future might change so radically that I am better off learning to be flexible than becoming attached to the way I think things will be.

It is more productive to think about what is within my control than to worry and fret about things that are outside of my control. Worrying is not a form of thinking.

Much of what happens is not worthy of my attention. Fads, fashions, celebrities, news, propaganda, advertising, politicians, and the like are meaningless ephemera. If I know how many things are unimportant in the world, I can focus on what is truly important in my own life.

27. To Choose and Not to Choose

Honoring the power of choice brings me great simplicity, but sometimes greater simplicity comes from not choosing.

Some choices are already made for me. I am what I am, and the challenge is to become what I can be, not to change myself fundamentally and completely.

Roark is described as a force of nature. Do I try to change the earth or the ocean or the sky? No, but I can harness them to achieve my values. Just so I can harness and direct and master myself. I am a unique combination of talents, interests, sensitivities, capacities, and potentials. Why attempt to overcome these things, when instead I can use them as the strong foundation for building my life?

Yet the things that I choose are the essence of my life. When I choose something, I accept it, affirm it, admire it, let it into my life, give it my living energy, say yes to it in a total, undivided way. It becomes part of me and I become as faithful to it as I am to myself.

28. To Act and Not to Act

Honoring the power of action brings me great mastery, but sometimes greater mastery comes from not taking action.

After Roark received his first commissions, his stream of clients dried up. Strangely, he did nothing. He went to his office every day and sat in silence and inactivity. Did he know that he had to wait patiently for the time when he could succeed?

There is a time for action and a time for inaction. Many things cannot be achieved directly. Can I directly achieve happiness, enlightenment, dignity, beauty? No. These are things that must be built slowly, over time. I can approach them only from the side, not head on. In the *Tao Te Ching*, this is called action through non-action.

29. To Feel and Not to Feel

Honoring the power of feeling brings me great depth, but sometimes greater depth comes from not feeling.

Just as worrying is not a form of thinking, so it is best to cast off many of the negative emotions of life. Yes, I can feel righteous in my anger, realistic in my pessimism, justified in my anxiety, alive in my misery or grief. Yet the essence of life is serenity, optimism, creation, energy, action, joy.

Does this path lead to repression? I once thought so, but now I see how unproductive it is to wallow in negative emotions. Notice how, even with those who wanted to destroy him, Roark did not hate others or fear them or get angry with them or let them cause him suffering, because that which is negative goes down only so deep and does not touch the essence of life. I can experience and accept such things without giving up the fundamental assertiveness of the life force within me, without giving up my positive right to happiness and beauty and fulfillment.

Knowing when not to feel gives me a peculiar sense of freedom — of being light, clean, unpressured, unburdened, self-contained, untainted by all that is ugly and small.

30. Yin and Yang

To live successfully, Howard Roark found it necessary to balance thinking and not thinking, choosing and not choosing, acting and not acting, feeling and not feeling — to balance what Chinese philosophers call the yin and the yang.

The yang is that which is more rational, Apollonian, objective, public, open, well-known, bright, scientific, logical, explicit, lucid, clear, hard, dry, airy, powerful, firm, active — that which is related to the sky gods, to high mountains, to Olympus.

The yin is that which is more emotional, Dionysian, subjective, private, personal, unknown, shadowy, humanistic, perceptual, implicit, tacit, opaque, soft, damp, watery, solid, yielding, passive — that which is related to the gods of land and water, to things that are earthy and oceanic.

To think clearly and rationally, to choose my values and focus on what I find important, to create great value and reshape the earth in the image of my values, even to be passionate about life — these, for Rand, are facets of the yang. Yet the yang is not everything. There are aspects of life that are irreducibly yin — the kinds of things that are hard to put into words but that instead must simply be experienced: music, painting, sculpture, dance, gardening, nature, manual labor, athletics, exercise, physicality, sensuality, breath, yoga, meditation, introspection, reflection, contemplation, reverence, awareness, perception, the senses, beauty, adornment, pleasure, relaxation, spontaneity, friendship, love.

These phenomena, these manifestations of yin, have their philosophies, too: Taoism, Buddhism, Epicureanism, aestheticism, gnosticism, organicism, naturalism, yogism, spiritualism, and more. These philosophies and practices can help me gain deep insights into the meaning of life.

The great challenge is to find unity in diversity, to achieve a harmony of opposites within myself, to attain a balance among the forces and qualities represented by the yin and the yang. This is not easy; indeed it is one of the supreme challenges of living. Yet I cannot climb that great mountain of wisdom if I am the hedgehog who knows only one big thing; instead, I must be the fox who knows many things and who has many ways of knowing. I must be open to experiencing life, to recognizing what I truly want — even if it appears to be at odds with the yang-like philosophy of Ayn Rand.

31. The Architecture of Happiness

The newspaper caption beneath a picture of Howard Roark standing before the Enright House reads: "Are You Happy, Mr. Superman?" The irony is that Mr. Superman is indeed happy, because making his values real by bringing beautiful buildings into the world is, for Roark, a source of the most exalted enjoyment one could imagine.

This level of joy is not mere fun or pleasure, but a deep alignment between my values and their realization in the world — a form of metaphysical joy or love for existence. Yet is such joy found only in the highest creations of the human spirit? Does joy require in all instances a feeling of man-worship or a heroic sense of life? No. For me, joy is the word that best captures a deeply positive, constructive, humanistic approach to life, work, art, love, family, friendship, and the pursuit of wisdom. This approach to life is built on the assumption that man is born to glory and that happiness is my sacred birthright.

Does honoring the power of thought require me to live up to an explicitly rational view of man and the universe in everything I think and do, or even to forsake passion? No. I live a life of reason when my actions are clear, intelligible, integrated, open to the fundamental human power of understanding myself and the world. But the power of understanding includes perception, imagination, and introspection as well as explicitly conceptual thought. As Jacob Bronowski wrote in his poem *The Abacus and the Rose*, I must "reject the feud of eye and intellect"; reason's hand, far from being cold and clammy, provides the touch that enables both light and heat, both thought and passion, both deep understanding and deep emotion. Joy and reason go hand in hand.

Finally, can meaning be realized only in the loftiest abstractions or most cosmic goals? Does the search for meaning mandate that I must take an explicitly philosophical approach to every aspect of my life? No. Meaning emerges through an interaction between my choices and my actions, in the self-directed achievement of what I have chosen as good or important. But the good and the important are not mere abstractions: they can be as particular as the smile of a friend, the scent of a flower, the sense of a phrase. Individuality extends that far; and meaning is found not merely in the cosmic and the universal, but also most directly in the concrete, in the particular, in the deeply personal, in what it closest to me: in the activities of my work, in the loving kindness of my family, in the support of my chosen friends, in the fellowship of the communities in which I live and act, in the irreplaceable health of my body, in the character that I build up within me, in my creative pursuits, in the ornaments of life that I enjoy in nature and human culture.

32. The Sovereign Individual

Roark said that thought, choice, action, and feeling are the functions of the self. In order to live a successful human life, I must be independent in my thinking, my choices, my actions, and my feelings. It is this independence that Roark possesses but that Keating lacks.

Independence gives me ultimate power over my own life. Not power over others, but power over myself: the inner strength to understand reality, to direct my energy and attention, to create value, to experience meaning.

To be independent in this way is to be a sovereign individual, to be a law-maker for myself, to be a self-governor.

This supreme independence makes me free.

33. A Higher Step

Supreme independence makes me free. But free for what? Is it enough merely to be free, to be without ties to the world, to govern myself in solitude and inactivity?

Roark's way of life says no.

Independence is but a precondition, which frees me to create great value, to make something that is an improvement upon nature instead of a degradation, to produce a higher step that would be impossible without human action in the world. It is this fundamental creativity that Roark possesses but that Toohey lacks.

A higher step is respectful of nature, just as Roark's structures respect the sites upon which they are built. It knows that nature has its own beauty, and it strives to add further beauty that even nature could not provide.

The principle of the higher step is a difficult taskmaster. It is much easier to blast away the granite of a mountain than to work with that granite to build a Heller House or a Monadnock Valley. It is also much easier to blast away the foundations of my personality and remake it in the image of Rand's philosophy than to engage in the more delicate task of self-improvement.

Is my work a higher step above what I have inherited from nature and tradition? Are my relationships higher steps above what my family and earlier generations have bequeathed to me? Is my soul a higher step above what nature and nurture have provided to me?

Independence frees me to create great value. It is up to me whether I make that potential real.

34. The Great Task

Why create value? Does the world deserve that effort from me? Doesn't creating great value place me at the mercy of the world? Wouldn't it be easier to seek power over the world so that it cannot harm me?

Here again, Roark's way of life says no.

In his job interview with Henry Cameron, Roark says that he doesn't like the shape of things and that he wants to change that shape through his own efforts, through the application of his own creative power — not through power over others. This purpose, expressed in architecture, is the great task of his life. It is just such a great task of value-creation that Roark possesses but that Wynand lacks.

Is it realistic for me to have the goal of reshaping the world in the image of my values? Not directly. But then all Roark did was design some buildings — it's not as if he reshaped the entire world. Instead, he made his values real in the world through the limited yet still significant scope of what was possible to him.

The ethical issue here is not the relative extent of what I can achieve in life compared to famous inventors, scientists, or artists, but the absolute extent of what I can achieve based on my interests, my talents, and the energy I can realistically expend on my most important projects and relationships during the brief span of my life on this earth. At that level, I too am capable of great things.

35. The Noble Soul

I am capable of great things. But it takes enormous discipline to truly understand the world and myself, to focus my energy and attention on what I find interesting and important, to create value in myself, in my relationships, and in my projects. It would be much easier to float through life and to depend on the achievements of others.

Yet to do so would be unworthy of a truly human being. If I abdicate my responsibilities and do not live up to my potential, then I forsake the birthright of a glorious, successful human life. Deeply positive thought, choice, action, and feeling are right and proper to a noble soul — and if I do not strive for nobility, why am I here?

36. The Spirit of Youth

Just as the boy on the bicycle was captivated by Monadnock Valley, so *The Fountainhead* appeals deeply to young people who seek joy and reason and meaning in life. Rand's novel is a confirmation of the spirit of youth, capturing the almost-painful sense of expectation with which a young person can enter into the greater world. Think of those in the courtroom as Roark takes the stand at his trial, who for a moment see him as he really is and who feel the same potential in themselves: independent, strong, capable, courageous, benevolent, clean, innocent, fearless, free.

Is that radiant picture an illusion? Do the curiosity and idealism of youth need to cool and harden into a passionless wisdom — energy and enthusiasm into a settled maturity — openness and flexibility into a cautious security — courage and daring into a conservative practicality?

Perhaps not.

Perhaps, instead, true security comes from self-reliance, from the strength of my skills, from the health of my body, from self-control and self-mastery, from limiting my needs and desires to what is natural and becoming of a liberated individual, from fellowship with chosen friends who honor the same values I do.

Perhaps true practicality comes from cultivating the deepest sense of who I am, from immersion in life, from an unwavering focus on what matters, from knowing the name of my soul.

Perhaps true maturity comes from holding onto the right ideals, from self-respect and respect for others, from a strong sense of personal responsibility, from continually improving myself, from becoming who I am and what I can be.

Perhaps true wisdom comes from the passionate search for passionless truth, from endlessly seeking new experiences, from always seeing the world with fresh eyes, from never succumbing to conventional categories or party lines, from being authentic and direct in my dealings with self and others.

37. Freedom

The Fountainhead is a novel of freedom.

This freedom is not political but personal: the freedom of self-reliance, of skill, of being capable of surviving and thriving in the world, of standing on my own two feet, of moving through life with strength and competence and independence.

This freedom is the positive liberty to do what matters — to create, to produce, to think, to choose, to act, to feel, to live.

This freedom is the liberation of holding nothing back from my life, of being fundamentally open to experience, of actively seeking after enlightenment, dignity, depth, and beauty.

This freedom is the true wealth of creativity, of friendship, of love, of doing what I truly want, of being what I aspire to be.

This freedom is the result of self-governance, self-mastery, and self-trust — for when I trust myself completely, I do not need to depend on some authority outside of myself and my own relationship to reality.

This freedom brings the ultimate security and leads to the ultimate serenity.

Yet this freedom can be approached only from the side. I cannot grasp it directly. It must grow within me and around me, through the decisions and actions I take every day, through the responsibilities I shoulder, through the powers I exercise. The liberation I experience is a sign of success, and results from the hard work of personal responsibility.

38. Dignity

In *Les Misérables*, Victor Hugo says that work makes one free and thought makes one worthy of freedom.

To be worthy of freedom is to have a fundamental dignity of soul.

Dignity means idealism without partisanship, self-possession without self-importance, purpose without anxiety, perspective without detachment. It means being thoughtful but not argumentative, steadfast but not stolid, serious but joyful, patient but not complacent, respectful but but not cold, quiet but not numb, active but not frenzied. It means strength, poise, style, and grace.

There is no substitute for personal dignity, and no standard of dignity except independence. Not the surface independence of fads and fashions, but independence where it matters most: the autonomy of my source of energy in life; being self-motivated and self-generated and self-sufficient in spirit; finding in myself, in my highest ideals, and my aspirations for excellence a first cause, a fount of energy, a life force.

Dignity, too, is a height that I can approach only gradually and indirectly. For what is dignity but worth, merit, character, excellence? These things emerge only in the fullness of time. I must grow into dignity through spiritual maturity, moral ambition, and creative aspiration over a span of many years.

39. Depth

The quality of the soul is in its depths, says the *Tao Te Ching*.

The hardest thing in the world is to know and do what I truly want, says *The Fountainhead*.

I cannot be content with the mere surface of life. I must explore its innermost depths, I must go to the heart of things, I must push beyond what is expected and necessary and average to achieve what is fine and great and rare. I must live without reservations and hold nothing back from life.

There is danger in living this way, and it takes courage to do so. Yet ultimately it is the most practical way to live because only by focusing on what truly matters can I be successful as a human being.

40. Beauty

When I am selective about how I live my life, I achieve a deep simplicity, an honesty and purity and austerity, a lack of pretension and hypocrisy, an ease and efficiency of choice and action, a timeless sense of calm focus, graceful proportion, and true integrity, a harmony of the parts of my life, a quiet but undeniable energy, a truth to myself, a moral excellence — even, at times, a share in the divine. What is this except beauty?

When I live in this way, I do justice to the real relation, the underlying theme, the ways of true humanity. I am rooted, centered, immersed, engaged, alive to wonder, at ease with life, at home on this earth, aligned with the beauty of existence. I have, too, a sense of lightness, a grace of motion and thought and action, a splendor in my daily routine, a lovely serenity that so easily becomes a smile directed at everything that is.

There is wisdom in selectivity, and beauty in that wisdom.

41. The Fountainhead

Roark is uniquely different because he consistently and fundamentally honors the fountainhead of human progress: the individual person whose self-nature is aligned with the human powers of thought, choice, action, and feeling, and therefore who has the courage to independently understand reality, to focus on what is important, to create great value in the world, and to experience the deep emotional meaning of life.

There is something primal and eternal about this fountainhead — it is an ever-flowing spring of upward movement, the ultimate source of human ingenuity and happiness, an inexhaustible well of energy, the life-force that has raised humanity in its ever-accelerating ascent, the deepest root of joy and reason and meaning in life. And this is so because the ground of all reality, the depth of all being, lies in individuality. Every thing and every being is individual by virtue of itself and nothing else.

Although this fountainhead is often obstructed and redirected, it can never be fully suppressed because it is latent in every human being as a divine spark of curiosity, a sacred fire of passion, a focused beam of attention, a molten source of energy. These qualities might sound sophisticated, but in fact they are utterly natural: for I am born into this world as a thinking, choosing, acting, feeling being, and when I grow up and out into the world I cannot help but wonder about what I see, turn my attention toward what interests me, care about some people and things more than others, and act to fulfill my needs and desires.

The question is not whether I will think and choose and act and feel, for exercising these powers is as natural as moving and breathing. The question is whether I will honor these innate powers in myself and in others, whether I will live a life of freedom, dignity, depth, and beauty, whether I will align my character with what is best in human nature, whether I will find joy and reason and meaning on this earth, whether I will live up to my highest potential and in so doing transform the latent fountainhead within me into a living reality.

42. The Life Force

The depth of all being lies in individuality, and the basis of all life lies in the energy of every living thing.

My living energy takes many forms: the mental energy of my thinking, the psychological energy of my attention, the physical energy of my actions, the emotional energy of my feelings, and other, more specific forms of energy within me.

At every moment of my existence, my life is defined by the energy I absorb, the energy I conserve, the energy I transform, and the energy I expend.

There are many external sources of energy in my life: the food I eat and drink, the air I breathe, the sunlight I soak up, the sights and sounds that impinge upon my senses, the things I buy and trade, the books I read, the art works I experience, the inspiration of witnessing the happiness and success of others, the attention I receive from my companions and friends and family. In all these domains of life, I can choose wisely or poorly.

The same is true of the ways I can conserve or waste the energy within me: my posture, my breathing, my sense of balance and proportion, my emotional self-control, my avoidance of negative thoughts and emotions, my honoring the wisdom of my body and my soul, and all the ways that I prepare my mind and body for the activities of life.

That which I take in and conserve is potential energy that I can transform into the kinetic energy of action: the work I do, the things I create, the people I love and support, and how I move through the hours and days and years of my life.

What is my life but this living energy, which I can harness and expend to create joy and reason and meaning? Indeed, just as Newton described physical force as mass times acceleration, I can measure the life force in everything I do as content times intensity: that which I have chosen to do multiplied by the energy, attention, and passion I bring to each activity.

This life force is mine to control, mine to master, mine to direct as I choose, and mine to expend as I think best. No one else has a right to one iota of my living energy, and I have no right to yours, for this life force is the essence of individuality for every living thing.

43. Love for Existence

In his job interview with Henry Cameron, Roark said: "I love this earth. That's all I love." Think of Roark's Stoddard Temple: slung low over the ground, like the outstretched arms of a great benediction and a silent acceptance of the earth and of all the things on this earth that cannot be changed.

Roark accepted and loved the fact that existence exists. What he accepted and loved above all was the wonderful fact of his own existence. He was simply and deeply glad to be alive.

When I love existence in this way, and especially when I love my own existence, I gain a new fire, a sense that my life is important, a feeling that my happiness is sacred, a dedication to realizing the best of my spirit, a loyalty to my highest potential. I work to live up to the radiant picture of what is possible to me. I accept as the first law of my life an inner demand to seek the best of myself. I come to know that to be happy is my first duty to myself. I seek out the extra quality that makes dreams so vivid, and I try to make that quality real in my waking hours.

When I love and accept this earth, I find that my daily routine can have honesty and dignity, that the routine necessities of life can be wrapped in splendor. And why not? Yes, the world can be ugly and small, but life can also be beautiful. It is supremely good to be alive on this life-giving earth and to feel every day the fresh wonder of an untouched world.

This magnificent appreciation for life is a source of the highest joy possible to human hearts. For what greater joy could there be but to focus on the most important things in my life?

44. The Light Within

Along with Roark, I love not only existence in general and my own existence in particular, but also my consciousness of all that exists. This consciousness takes many forms: an abiding pleasure in the senses; a love of unadorned awareness; a desire to be actively present in my every interaction; a passionate search for knowledge, insight, discernment, and true perception; the wisdom to know the difference between what I can and cannot change.

To be conscious is to watch myself, to monitor myself, to work hard to overcome the things inside me that resist self-knowledge and self-awareness: the ever-present desire to go through life as if asleep, to deceive myself, to live in unconsciousness and darkness. It is to light the lamp of reason within me and to use that lamp to find the source of all reality, which is individuality — not only the singularity of my own existence but also that of every other person, living being, and physical thing.

As expressed in a beautiful image from the Gnostic Gospels, to be conscious is to knock upon myself as upon a door to a wider and brighter truth, to walk upon myself as upon a road to a higher plateau of awareness. It is to have a root and a center and a purpose. It is to know who I am, where I come from, and where I am going. It is to find the place of life and the name of my soul. It is to become my own best teacher and counselor, to accept my own mind as the father of truth, to seek no authority higher than myself and no value higher than my own judgment of what is right.

I cultivate the light within myself so that I can achieve spiritual maturity, personal enlightenment, and transformed awareness. If I do not cultivate the light of reason, I will not shine forth for myself or for those I care about; and if I do not shine forth, I will live in darkness.

45. The Meaning of Life

The meaning of life is not awareness, but action. As Roark said: "We live in our minds, and existence is the attempt to to bring that life into physical reality, to state it in gesture and form."

As Jesus said in the Gnostic Gospels: "If you bring forth what is within you, what you bring forth will save you. If you do not bring forth what is within you, what you do not bring forth will destroy you."

It is not enough to see and love the depth of all existence, nor enough to reason about what is great in life. I must also reach for what is highest, I must make the most of what I am and what I have, I must do my best to live up to what is good. I must aspire to constant improvement, to excellence, to whatever share of perfection I can achieve on this earth.

To stand where I am is nothing; but if I have the courage to change what I can and if I am able to reach the final expression of my highest possibility, then I will be proud to stand in the place I have reached.

Too many people die a little each day. I must aspire to live more each day. For the higher I aim and the higher I reach, the more my life is truly mine.

Just as Roark's Heller House grew from the cliff on which it was built, as if the cliff had completed itself through the building of the house — so I aspire to grow from what I was and to complete myself through the building of my character and my life. If I do so, I will have a strong foundation, I will have a root and a center and a purpose. And if I achieve this I will not be swayed by others, I will not be buffeted by the winds of circumstance, I will refuse to measure myself against others or as merely a part of some group or movement or tradition. I will live first-hand.

Just as no building must copy another, so no person must copy another. My life is made by own needs. I base my self-respect on the highest standards of personal achievement. I seek not to rule and I seek not to teach; I seek only to build and to create whatever value I can bring forth during my all-too-brief time on this beautiful earth. My most searching goals and achievements are not universal and other-directed and social, but personal and self-motivated and not to be touched.

What is the use and the meaning of my life? I am the use and the meaning.

46. The Way

It is said in the *Tao Te Ching*: the way that can be walked is not the eternal way; the name that can be named is not the eternal name.

Some take this in a mystical sense, but my interpretation is more practical: the eternal way is general, but the way that I can walk is individual; the eternal name is universal, but the name of my soul is mine alone.

Roark's way, too, was his alone. When I first immersed myself in *The Fountainhead*, I thought that I must live as Roark lived. Yet my path is individual: I might not know my calling at the age of ten, as Roark knew he wanted to be an architect; I might by nature be more social than Roark, more collaborative, more lighthearted, more conventional in some respects; I might express my creative powers in different ways, perhaps through mastering a craft or pursuing a hobby or providing an excellent service or nurturing those I care about or building an organization or maintaining what has been created by others. If so, I must know and accept the name of my soul and use those strengths to find my own way in life.

This supreme respect for the individual is something beyond a mere intellectual assent to a philosophy of individualism in the abstract. Instead, it is a pure love for individuality in all its manifest particulars — my own individuality, your individuality and that of each person I interact with, the individuality of each being, each thing, each place, each project, each task, each performance, each perception, each moment in time.

When I experience individuality so completely, I live more fully each day because I am always encountering something new and special and uniquely valuable. Each moment that I am blessedly alive, I feel the fresh wonder of an untouched world and I come to know more deeply the path that I alone can walk.

47. This White Serenity

In the *Tao Te Ching*, *te* is precisely this individuality: self-nature, raw personhood, character, intention, quality, worth, personal actuality or singularity — good or bad, positive or negative, it is what I am. By contrast, *tao* is human nature, the one path, the great way, a constraining track, an endless course of forward motion, even cosmic unity or potentiality. The tension between individuality and generality, between self-nature and human nature, between actuality and potentiality, between what I am and what I could be, between the way that I can walk and the eternal way, is one of the great themes of life.

In *The Fountainhead*, the most dramatic conflict is not between Roark and Keating or Toohey or Wynand, but between Roark and Dominique. She is like *te* — raw, strange, unconstrained, unbridled, singular, Rand herself in a bad mood. He is like *tao* — self-consistent, unified, integrated, unstoppable, a force of nature. There is a great tension between them, an inexplicable violence that I find unsettling and mystifying unless viewed metaphorically.

Yet at the end of the novel, Roark and Dominique achieve a white serenity that is the sum of all the violence they have known — just as the tension between *te* and *tao*, the struggle between myself and the great way, the sometimes difficult dance between my individuality and the underlying track of right living, is harmonized through experience and reflection, action and understanding, ceaselessly applying the life energy of my being, and patiently waiting for knowledge to settle into hard-won wisdom within me.

What is the alignment between *te* and *tao* but philosophy, the love of wisdom made real in my life? Such a philosophy is not a dry subject for bookish learning. It is, as Thoreau said in *Walden*, to solve some of the problems of life, not just theoretically but practically. It is my ongoing relationship with wisdom and insight and right living. It is the one path to being successful as a human being, to living in a way that is consistent with true humanity. Achieving that alignment brings a great calmness of spirit, the simplicity of being at home on this earth, the ability to feel completely natural, a sense of freedom in serenity, the quiet radiance of certainty, of innocence, of peace with the world and of peace within myself. This white serenity is knowing and returning to the source, to the fountainhead of joy and reason and meaning in life, to my own individuality.

48. The Tao of Roark

The heart of the earth is made of fire, but sometimes it breaks through and shoots out to freedom. One such spark is Roark's Wynand Building. Another is *The Fountainhead* itself.

In the final scene of *The Fountainhead*, Dominique visits Roark at the construction site for the Wynand Building. Riding the elevator to the top, she passes the pinnacles of bank buildings:

> My life is more than finance and economics, more than my career, more than the money I earn. Money is only a means to some personal purpose of my choosing — to invest, to create, to study, to enjoy my limited time on this earth, to live as I see fit. I seek not the power of wealth, but the power of creation. When I let go of money as my primary motivation, I become truly prosperous.

She crests the crowns of courthouses:

> My life is more than law and politics, more than my interactions with others, more than my contributions to society. The life of society is secondary, whereas the life of the individual is primary and sacred. If I look to others for fulfillment, I will never be fulfilled. I seek not to rule or to govern, but to create and to build. When I let go of making laws for others, I become more honest, more simple, more direct, more free.

She rises above the spires of churches:

> My life is more than religion or philosophy, more than my adherence to a system of ideas, even if that system was created by Ayn Rand herself. I seek not to teach, but to know; and I know that what matters is not to

repeat the words of the tao, but to embody it and live it. When I believe in myself and in my own highest potential, I no longer need to convince others of what I believe. When I let go of Rand's system as I would to a ladder that has helped me to climb higher and see farther, I become serene.

And then there was only the ocean and the sky and the figure of Howard Roark:

> My life is mine to live and enjoy, my individuality is the only untouchable constant of my existence, joy and reason and meaning are not an impossible ideal but a natural way of living that is mine to discover, mine to choose, mine to achieve, and mine to enjoy. My supreme possessions are not outside of me but within me: my integrity, my honor, my freedom, my ideals, my convictions, the honesty of my feelings, the independence of my thoughts, the name of my soul.

That way of living is what I call the Tao of Roark:

> It is not the tao of Roark only, but my tao and your tao, the source of all joy and reason and meaning, the fountainhead of individual freedom, personal dignity, spiritual depth, and moral beauty. Although I draw deeply from the well of individuality, it is never used up because it is always full within me. Even when I think I have lost it, I must realize that it can neither be lost nor found, for it is the center and the essence of life, the singing answer to the promise of the music of youth, and a consecration to a joy that justifies the earth.

THE END

For Further Exploration

This book was over thirty years in the making. I first read *The Fountainhead* at the age of thirteen, read it eight more times in the following five years, then went about the task of trying to live a good human life.

Yet *The Fountainhead* was always within me, even when I explored wisdom traditions far removed from Ayn Rand: Epicurus, Nietzsche, Thoreau, Aristotle, Lao Tzu, even the gnostic Jesus. Eventually I plan to write books about each of them; until then I recommend my Epicurean dialogue *Letters on Happiness* (the second book in this series of philosophers on happiness), Walter Kaufmann's translation of Nietzsche's *Gay Science*, Thoreau's *Walden*, Joe Sachs' translation of Aristotle's *Nicomachean Ethics*, Derek Lin's translation of the *Tao Te Ching*, and *The Gnostic Gospels* by Elaine Pagels.

The most direct musical inspiration for *The Tao of Roark* is Bach's *Goldberg Variations*, of which my favorite versions are Glenn Gould's second recording on piano and Catrin Finch's recent recording on harp.

A book is a point reached; yet it is not the last word. If you would like to explore the ideas in *The Tao of Roark*, feel free to visit my website at https://stpeter.im/ or to contact me using the information posted there.

9780615822952